The Guru of Marketing

The Guru of Marketing

A Handbook Simplifying Marketing in the 21st Century.

Ramblings which might help practitioners
at the beginning of their career.

JAY NAYAR

authorHOUSE®

AuthorHouse™
1663 Liberty Drive
Bloomington, IN 47403
www.authorhouse.com
Phone: 1-800-839-8640

© 2013 by Jay Nayar. All rights reserved.

No part of this book may be reproduced, stored in a retrieval system, or transmitted by any means without the written permission of the author.

Published by AuthorHouse   01/14/2013

ISBN: 978-1-4817-8106-0 (sc)
ISBN: 978-1-4817-8107-7 (e)

Any people depicted in stock imagery provided by Thinkstock are models, and such images are being used for illustrative purposes only. Certain stock imagery © Thinkstock.

This book is printed on acid-free paper.

Because of the dynamic nature of the Internet, any web addresses or links contained in this book may have changed since publication and may no longer be valid. The views expressed in this work are solely those of the author and do not necessarily reflect the views of the publisher, and the publisher hereby disclaims any responsibility for them.

Contents

The Book of Relationships 1
Book II: Book Of Service 13
Book III: The Book of Value...................................... 25
Book IV: The Book of Divisions 29
Book V: The Book of Competition 35
Book of Trends 49
Book VII: Finer Points for Competition and
    the Marketer... 53
Book VIII: Buyer Psychology 61
Book IX: On the Marketer-Psyche: Of
    Hope and Fear 69
Book X: The Learning Marketer...............................75

The Book of Relationships

1. This is the Marketing Command, this is the Marketing Teaching, this is the Marketing Element, and this you shall observe: There is only one *chant*: *Be customer centric.*
2. Market is a targeted *group of customers*. Your target group could be mass or class, depending on your product or service.
3. The very *purpose* of your organization's existence is the *customer*. The organization ceases to exist without the customer. All organizational life originates with the creation of a customer.
4. Organizations seek profits. Customers seek *value*. The means to organizational profits is to exchange positive values with the customer.
5. The motto of organizational success is: to *win with* the customer. Both parties must gain positive values for a meaningful relationship

and the aggregate must indicate a bigger gain.
6. There is synergy in the commonality of interests between the organization and its customer.
7. Your objective as a customer service representative is to satisfy the customer through the fulfillment of the customer's needs.
8. Needs are the fundamental yearnings of the customer; it is the basic requirements originating in the human mind.
9. A customer *'wants'* your services or products merely to satisfy these fundamental *'needs'*. A need emanates from the deeper cravings in the customer; it affords you an opportunity to serve him. The want is a manifestation of the need.
10. Do not speculate to know; or presume you understand the needs of your customer straightaway; appearances may be deceptive: conduct an in depth exploration to study need; to do so you *need* to have infinite patience.
11. The customer does not *want* your product, he only *seeks to satisfy his need.*

12. Try to understand the need of the customer rather than try to satisfy his wants.
13. The customer sees you as a potential problem—solver, a 'problem fixer'.
14. Know your limits: the customer seeks you out in order to satiate his need and thus obviate his problem. The need begets the demand for services or products as such.
15. It is *'myopic'* to believe that a transaction is a transient deal or a one-time deal. A transaction is the beginning of a perpetual relationship.
16. A *continuum of exchanges* establishes a marketer's relationship with his customer. Every relation has a motive. One may not be able to decipher all of the motives of the customer.
17. One cannot attempt to change a *customer's motive*. This is a constraint that exists.
18. The customer evaluates each one of these exchanges and views you through the prism of his view based on his experiences.
19. Marketing life is about relationships. Successful life is about successful relationships.

20. Build relationships with your customers. Build bridges with them. See every interaction as a brick laid in the bridge to your customer.
21. See every transaction as a *'moment of truth'* as Jan Carlson said several years ago.
22. At the end of every interaction, there ought to be a sense of satisfaction for both parties if there must be a continuum in the relationship.
23. Your client perceives the marketing function from his perspective. Do not endeavour to alter that perspective.
24. Exceed his expectations if you can; work towards a *'wow'*; if that is not possible at least match his expectations. You have to manage a customer's expectations.
25. The customer's expectation matches your service: customer evaluates in congruence (satisfaction), null congruence (dissatisfaction) or positive congruence (exceedingly satisfied).
26. Understanding the customer requires that you have a prior understanding of the environment in which you operate.

27. It is important to recognize that fundamentals of the environment like economic, political, socio-cultural or regulatory factors influence the environment.
28. The environment is also swayed by technical factors; a digital world makes life simultaneously easier and difficult.
29. The customer is a sentimental human being: handle him like glass. He is likely fragile.
30. Your offer affects customer; the customer's response affects your product or services. There is mutuality of interests and inter-dependence.
31. 'Publics' are crucial for success in marketing. Identify the components of publics relevant for you and your offerings.
32. A 'public' for you is any stakeholder who has a stake in your organization.
33. Be alert to the environment, and to its public constituents to capture the essence of your competitor's strengths, opportunities, threats and weaknesses. To be alert is to scan the environment.
34. Scanning implies deep, silent inner reflection on yourself and on your organization.

35. During the scan, assess yourself and your organization for its pillars and rusted girders.
36. Build on your strengths; reduce your weaknesses. This is an essential pre-requisite to strategize for an appropriate market share.
37. Your competitors move ahead on various tactics: they may use prices, product feature differentiation, variations in distribution channels, and enthusiasm in promotion efforts—to your detriment.
38. In a technologically advanced world, choice of technique is a means to establishing a relationship with the customer. 'Bricks and mortar' is less relevant in modern times as compared to 'mouse and—click'.
39. The distribution network in most cases is technology driven today. Technology is not a constant; it is a dynamic accompaniment to marketing.
40. Speed of a transaction is of essence to the consumer. Speed has to be coupled with accuracy.

41. If you, your product or your organization is perceived as obsolete, then you might have a shrinkage of market space.
42. Your frontiers are a shifting market. You are always in an unstable equilibrium. You have to try to balance within a constraint system.
43. Know the new boundaries in today's global markets and work out a strategy to stay afloat.
44. Organizations have to be on a learning curve to comprehend the essence of market dynamics.
45. Your transactions are here and now. You are engaged with the customer in the immediate short run.
46. A series of immediate short run marketing interaction cycles make a long run cycle. Engagement with the customer in the long run is only possible if you are engaged in the short run. All action that makes a relationship exist over the long term begins with your approach in the short run.
47. Educating the customer of our product or service is an investment not a cost. It may

be an investment even to educate a non customer.
48. Know whom you are expected to serve; you are their subject.
49. Before you set out to know your customer [KYC] know your organization's mission, vision, and values.
50. To serve your customer, you must be result oriented and producing internal resources.
51. Lofty ideals need to be backed up with an ability to back up internally. Your front office is just as strong as your back office is.
52. Discover your core competencies. You have to be competent to meet organizational goals. Equip yourself.
53. Deliver on your promises. If you do not have the ability to deliver, do not promise.
54. Ask yourself these few questions, which are perhaps the most simple:
    - What business are we in?
    - Where are we now?
    - What do we need to grow?
    - Can we change? How do we do that?
      The simplest questions are sometimes the most difficult to answer.

55. A customer has selective retention and selective amnesia: he retains only that which he wants to remember.
56. A client may have short memory on a positive experience. By contrast, negative episodes linger and hurt. If there are unpleasant interactions, he remembers them most.
57. If there is a service lapse or a product fault, then the client retains powerful [and detrimental to you] memory.
58. In exchanges with your customer, thus positive begets positive. Negative begets negative multifold.
59. If one of the two parties in a relationship is dissatisfied, then the transaction is incomplete. It means a sub-optimal point in the customer's expectations.
60. Customers remember interruptions to transactions more than the transactions themselves.
61. Every customer expects tender, loving care. (TLC)
62. Every customer is unique: no standard solutions can be applied across the board. Sizes differ from small to xxl.

63. Meeting client expectations is about understanding revealed consumer preferences. They reveal preferences in a coy manner.
64. Customer trades off in his mind continuously between benefits and the price he pays for that product or service; this is his estimation of returns on his fund outlay (R-P); we may call this as the consumer's estimated surplus.
65. You are trading off continuously between price that you will obtain from the market and the costs involved (P-C). This we call the producer's estimated surplus.
66. As P and—P cancel out the essence of value in any transaction is the differences between the estimated returns for the customer and the cost he incurs. [R-C] Maximum returns at least costs is what the customer really seeks. The returns need not be monetary but might include non monetary rewards too.
67. Consumers could reveal their preferences in some subtle form. Your success depends on your comprehension of such revealed preferences.

68. Marketing is not a slogan or a billboard; it is a string on which transactions are knit together in several strands of divergent moments of interactive truth.
69. Each customer interface is a rare occasion to solidify your series of interactions. The customer measures it mentally even as he experiences it.
70. That experience for the customer is the truth. Make every moment memorable. What is truthful is memorable.
71. Reinforce good memories continually for the customer. Make him feel good.
72. Walk the talk. If your post sales support does not support your offer, your customer feels betrayed.
73. Any unilateral success on your part at the cost of the customer is victory in the short run but pyrrhic in the long run.
74. Markets permit only normal gain. Abnormal gains are aberrations.
75. Undue gains on a customer and consequential deviant profits today are foregone normal profits of tomorrow.

76. In case we make abnormal returns we need to investigate the cause for such high returns from a customer. Skimming off is a tactic, not a strategy.

    Profits take time to arrive at your doorstep. You have to serve, stand and wait for profits.

77. A customer operates in a constraint system where hew assigns weights to priorities. Comprehend these priorities: Trust building between you and the customer; 7 Ps (Product, Prices, Promotion, People, Packaging, Positioning); 4 Cs (Customers, Competitors; Capabilities); 4 Rs (Relationships; Repetition; References; Recovery).

Book II

Book Of Service

Felt in the blood, and felt along the heart; and passing even into my purer mind with tranquil restoration—feelings too of unremembered pleasure . . .

William Wordsworth

1. Let your customer behold the many splendours and hues of your service in amazement.
2. The needs of a customer are multi-dimensional. They are dynamic and perennially on a change momentum. Keep pace.
3. Organizations are permanent; customers have therefore to be permanent. If customers are temporary and organizations are permanent, there is the likelihood of a structural mismatch.
4. Retain your customer. Let him return to you unhesitant. Loyalty is profits; profits follow

effective service. Service is Value. Value is Profits. S=V; V= P; therefore S= P.

5. You cannot serve the customer alone. Build your team around you to be as good as you.
6. Service implies quality. Quality implies value. Value implies profits. So all profits commence and end with good quality service.
7. Service is a team effort. There has to be substantive team support to your offer value when you engage the customer.
8. Relationship management is helped by Information Technology. Data base is about telecommunication plus communication plus people. Customer measures you in quadrants of technology and people.
9. Old customers are like old trees: they give us greater shades of profits. The longer the roots of the tree, the less the water that is needed.
10. Retaining customers is a more cost-effective proposition than adding on new ones.
11. Being efficient is about resources being used to good advantage. It is about input output relationships: less for more. You have to be efficient to be effective.

12. Being effective is about utilizing your abilities to the customer's advantage. However efficient you are, the customer needs to find you effective. You are only as good as the customer thinks you are.
13. You have to be knowledgeable to be efficient. You may be knowledgeable but may fail to deliver appropriately if you are not effective.
14. Nostalgia brings in loyalty. Your effort should be to bring in nostalgia. Be in his 'evoked' set; the customer should think of you spot-on in his hour of need. Work your way to his mind and may be even to his heart. He should be your champion.
15. Sensitivity is of essence in marketing. Be sensitive to the moment. Be sensitive to the person.
16. Customers expect a certain dedication to themselves. Indulge them professionally.
17. Care not just for your customer but be concerned about your non-customer too. Ask yourself as to why the non-customer is not switching loyalty to you.

18. Relationship is building one long bridge between you and the customer. Construct it through communication.
19. Periodically maintain the bridge. Over this infrastructure, you and the customer travel several times over.
20. Repetitious travel is self fulfilling and profitable. It has demonstrative value and one obtains a larger share of the customer's deals and purse.
21. Remember, the customer gets the right of way on the bridge always.
22. Humility is of essence in marketing. Like the ocean that receives the waters of all the rivers, you shall lie lower than the customer.
23. Humility encourages feedback. Feedback is learning. Learning is growth.
24. Creating a good customer profile is important in maintaining relationships; updating it regularly is even more important.
25. Services are intangible; they cannot be seen or touched but they are experienced, they touch the customer's mind and heart.
26. Services vary from one point of time to another. The many moods of the service

provider may affect services. The customer can afford to be moody. You cannot be.

27. Services are temporal. Services cannot be stored. They are here and now. They are perishable. You create them in them in the presence of the customer. You are influenced by his presence. Do not be overawed but be mutual.

28. Treat customers as a candle: protect them from the wind. Handle services delicately.

29. A customer may not be so expressive or revealing; he may not be ostensibly communicative. Use the enthusiasm of your service to reach out to him. Listen; draw him out. Listen, as the Chinese say, to the fall of the sunray on the earth.

30. Relationships are fathomless. In the depths of the caves of the ocean of relationship, there are gems of experience and treasure for profit. Every dive into the depths yields stones which these unfathomed caves of ocean have.

31. Concentrate on the customer rather than on selling your product. You cannot deliver to a person unless you have an interest in him.

32. The customer is conscious of his image and his self.
33. The customer seeks opinion and is influenced by opinion from others. Know his influence locales. It could be his spouse, kids, friends or groups he belongs to. Comprehend him and the influencers. Market to them.
34. The client might refer to social, symbolic or peer groups based on his identity, sense of belonging, religion or ethnicity. You have to observe and appreciate his group (segment) and accordingly tailor your offerings.
35. You have the right to give your opinion only if you are competent, to advise. A healthy relationship is founded on mutual respect.
36. Never fall in love with your viewpoint. If the customer has not entered into a deal, despite your best advice, be non-attached. Search for another deal.
37. Make every transaction a durable and a memorable one for the client. Services can perish; but relationships should not. Good services are indestructible and ivory pieces for the customer; they are carved in the customer's memory.

38. Organization is the means; you are the provider of the resource for the means and the customer's needs the end.
39. A customer is tied to you by the tenuous thread of good, quality driven service.
40. Customers are real. Customers may occasionally appear unreasonable: differences of opinion or unreasonableness are an illusion that has to be withered.
41. A world without a customer is unreal: *'of the unreal, there is no existence. Of the real, there is no non-existence'*. (Indian adage)
42. The final truth in the relationship is the triumph of the real and the abandonment of the unreal. Promote the real. Shed the unreal.
43. To err is human. It could be that you deliver weak; poor customer service may pass; good service should recover lost ground. Recovery through immediate corrective action is crucial to retention.
44. Every customer has the right to dream. A customer's financial abilities may not immediately be on display. His longing may

not be backed up by abilities. You have to be patient and lead him gently to his match.
45. Be original and innovative in your thoughts and actions.
46. Let the customer marvel at your profound words and sincere actions.
47. Empathy should come naturally to the marketer. We are dealing with the animate and the animate need compassion.
48. Listen to your customer like a prince; for a prince shall hear the blossoming of the flower. The prince of marketing shall hear the unheard. *'Heard melodies are sweet, those unheard are sweeter'.(Keats)* Develop a rare insight into customer requirements.
49. Various customers are on various rungs on the ladder of needs. Analyze their stage on the hierarchy and match them.
50. Customers seek safety, belongingness, social esteem or similar in their dealings. Give them the comfort and reassurance through your service.
51. Relationships cannot exist in disharmony. Harmonization is the aim.

52. Relationships cannot thrive in complexity. Relationships thrive in simplicity. The customer is simple-minded: do not befuddle him with terminology.
53. An experienced marketer always renders the counter-party at ease.
54. In any interaction, the customer becomes aware of the surroundings of the transaction and the visual experiences of the objects. So the ambience has to be right. The physical evidence matters. Bring cheer not opulence.
55. Invert your pyramid: you are the least important. Customers should come in first; they are your leaders; you follow them; do not lead them. Leading them is selling, not marketing.
56. The best organizational structures are those where the customer, not the organizational hierarchy decides the pecking order.
57. Structures must be customer responsive not wooden. The processes must be customer oriented. Rigidity is repellent.
58. Convey a bonded relationship. Express, manifest a genuine concern.

59. The delivery effort is a grand coalition within the organization, the internal customers of the organization and the actual customer whom the organization intends to serve.
60. Confrontation with a customer is against the code of beliefs in marketing.
61. The customer expects order and clarity in the processes.
62. Every interaction is relatively unique from the angle of communication; communication is the key to success in a relationship.
63. Communication is not about cajoling people to buy but it is seeking out their needs silently and genuinely trying to satisfy them.
64. Silence could be a depth indicator and a strong signal in communication.
65. In communication, a marketer has to be motivational and objective.
66. A marketing style is only as strong as its communication style.
67. Communication is beyond words. A customer detects subtle hints. He would see through prejudices and subjectivity. Avoid biases.

68. Communication must have *logos, pathos and ethos* in it: it must have logic, culture and feeling.
69. In communication, distance conveys meaning. Bodies co-operate at angles. Customers expect quick, accurate and deft moves.
70. End any interaction memorably. Customers remember the conclusion more.
71. Occasional rituals please the customer. Remembering anniversaries is good. Invitations for events makes him belong.
72. Do not let the customer be on the defensive. No one, least of all a client likes to be under duress in a meeting or in a conversation. Devise relaxation techniques as good starters.
73. There are no rules against defection by customers. If you give the customer a reason to leave, he will.
74. If your competitor gives the customer more in value, as he perceives it, he is tempted to switch.
75. Being level-headed and rational is essential in business. There will be profits in some deals and possible failures in others.

Balance between triumph and failure is essential. Equanimity is the quintessence of a marketer.

76. A marketer lives between hope and fear. You cannot make all of the profits all of the time but can make most of the profits in some of the time. Seasonality exists. Recessions exist. Peaks and trough exist. Festivals mark good times.

77. The fruit of marketing is the realization of past actions and services. The marketer's right is to act and act only; the results in relationship come much later. *Ad hocism* is not a good tactic.

78. That relationship in customer service is best which rises above the mundane.

79. The 'feel good' factor is important in any transaction. Pleasantness of feeling springs from good service. People need to feel encouraged to make a marketing decision.

Book III

The Book of Value

1. The customer is subject to influence. He is not a Robinson Crusoe.
2. He exists in the market within his society. Know your customer's society.
3. The Customer is simultaneously a part of several micro groups. He would also be a part of a large macro group.
4. Your ability to identify these reference groups helps you structure and position your offer as value to the customer.
5. Price is important for the customer; but he attaches more significance to value—the benefits he derives from a given product or service at a given price.
6. The customer attaches himself to an organization that offers him what he perceives as comparative value. You have to evidence value in all its deals.
7. A customer seeks value at the given price.

8. There is a trade—off between quality and price received.
9. To assess his trade—off level, you have to observe what attributes he values and then lay out the significance of these attributes to him.
10. Based on such mental valuation, see how your client differentiates you. Be aware that you are benchmarked.
11. The customer values a tradition for respecting excellence in your organization.
12. Most customers are eager for new technology in the new e-world. Customers often believe they need to be 'post—modern'. At least they expect the service providers to be post modern.
13. When customers are consistently unhappy with the value received, they exit. There are no huge barriers to exit while there may be barriers to entry.
14. Retaining a customer is always less costly than gaining a new one. So, if they leave, you have to reason why; build fortresses of goodwill to avoid exodus.

15. A value proposition is about all your promises to the consumer.
16. Your delivery system is part of the value system.
17. Satisfaction is a measurement between *point a and point b: a* being expectations and *b* being actuality. It is all about *ex ante* and *ex poste*. Performance narrows the gap.
18. Quality is about the satiating properties of the product and service.
19. The connectivity between satisfaction and loyalty differs according to individual proclivities of customers.
20. Look to lifetime value of a customer. (LTV) There is no short term.
21. Customer defection or churn is about negative value.
22. Check out the elasticity of demand to changes in price. People might endure price changes for quality delivered.
23. You could under-price and capture more market space or improve benefits to over-price. You should have an awareness of strategy to capture market space and to have higher margins.

24. A customer is willing to pay more for less if he sees value. Increase your benefits.
25. Experience reduces costs.
26. Every action has a reaction. Your competitor will respond to your price move very much as you would.
27. Markets are contestable. You could have an unpredicted competitor 'hit and run' with profits if you keep prices too high.
28. Discounts entice away from competitors in a falling market. Sell in a falling market with discounts.
29. Skimming is a one period gain; you must take advantage of a market situation recognizing that you are a multi-period incumbent.
30. Coordinating with your competitor may earn you lesser market space but higher margins. The regulators may frown on such coordination.
31. Response lags to price variations by your competitor.
32. Do not be frozen in the past.

Book IV

The Book of Divisions

(Divide to Multiply)
I took the one less traveled by, and that has made all the difference.

Robert Frost

1. Positioning for you is placing the customer before self. It is also placing you at a vantage point to seize an opportunity to market as it comes by.
2. Positioning for the customer is fixing an image about you in his mind. This is crucial for sustaining the relationship.
3. Discernible collaboration with the internal customer—your peers and colleagues—portrays you better in the minds of the customer.
4. Pareto's principle could be at work: 20 percent of your customers could bring in 80 percent of the profits. Cater to these

privileged few. *"All are equal but some are more equal"*. (Orwell)

5. A pool of the lesser privileged may also be a meaningful segment.
6. It could well be that the Pareto Principle might apply in your environment: 80 percent of your organization's work may be done by 20 percent of the staff. Be in the top percentile yourself.
7. Segment them customers on the basis of most profitable, profitable, low profitability and non profitable.
8. You have to apply varying standards among customers for convenience. A focus on high value potential customers may reduce transaction costs apart from the psychological lift that you confer on them.
9. Cluster them customers and focus on each cluster.
10. The customer is a social animal. People naturally cluster around groups and communities—tribalism, (called market segments) is real. Encouraging marketing tribalism reaps profits.

11. Segmentation must be scientific and must stand scrutiny. Segments must be significant, measurable, and viable in size; they ought to be accessible.
12. Ability to buy and willingness to buy are crucial elements to assess if it is a profitable segment. "The wise man sees not the same tree as the fool does"(Aldous Huxley).
13. Segmentation is steady discrimination. Segmentation is about division; this division is to multiply your profits.
14. Segments are worthwhile only if they return profits in the long run.
15. Strategy recognizes divisions with respect. Segmenting the population on variables helps carve *niche* (exclusive) markets.
16. However sincere and eager you are, you cannot serve all of your customers. Division of clientele based on common characteristics helps build values.
17. The market is far too wide: there could be those who struggle and those who are beyond materialism. Pick up your group well.

18. Personalities are different. Lifestyles are different.
19. Generations behave differently, shop differently. Grey hair behaves differently from black. Workmen shop differently from factory owners. Neighbourhoods matter.
20. Different groups require different approaches.
21. Higher income group clients have higher savings' potential: the marginal propensity to save is higher for high net worth customers.
22. The lower income groups could be an equally significant mass of resources if pooled together.
23. Encouraging the meek could be a remunerative strategy in a mass based product.
24. Your mass or class orientation is dependent on the product or services you offer.
25. Aggregation is appropriate if that yields benefit to you.
26. Non-sophisticated segmentation could be based on matters such as volume of purchases, method of conducting the deal—(e.g. non—cash based)

27. Price sensitivity and bargaining power are used to negotiate delivery obligations.
28. Some organizations use an undifferentiated strategy with their mass products' offerings. It might have a concentrated strategy when it comes to focusing on certain groups.
29. Organizations are well set on path to use a differentiated strategy when it deals with high net worth customers.
30. Comprehending an organization's current and probable future segments is important for the marketer.
31. Explore if there are other segments that you think have value-adding potential for your business.
32. Assess whether the patterns of market segmentation might change over time.
33. Study the impacting of resources and competencies required to perform well over different segments that your business targets or might target in the future.
34. Look into the segments which competitors focus on, or perform relatively better.

Book V

The Book of Competition

Begin and Cease, and then Again begin:
Matthew Arnold

1. If you are not aware where you are headed for, then you cannot ask your customer to join you on your journey.
2. The market is egged on by rivalry. Identify your rival. Know your competitor.
3. Recognize the key forces at work in the competitive environment of your business.
4. Work out how you would price your product *vis-a-vis* your competitor.
5. Developing a strategy is an attempt through deliberate planning, to meet organizational objectives.
6. Business goals may mean a combination of items such as revenue; market share; lowering costs; service; adding value; profit; and quality.

7. Today's 'globalized' market calls for innovative and breakthrough marketing strategies.
8. Trends influence markets. Mega trends influence markets in a major way.
9. Competitors influence you to change strategies. Peer pressure keeps you on toes. Substitution threats could emerge from new technologies.
10. Customers are an integral part of the change framework, they influence you to change.
11. Competitors stand influenced in relation to these competitive forces.
12. Marketer has to study the strengths and weaknesses in relation to the key forces at work of competitors.
13. To overcome competition, organizations need to attempt to influence the competitive forces affecting a business. This is not always possible.
14. Collusion with a competitor is illegal but cooperation is permissible.
15. In competitive markets, consumers are price sensitive. Sellers are closer to marginal costs.

16. You need to analyze and record the essential elements that impinge on the performance of your competitor.
17. Sustain client feedback. Obtain a feedback from your non-client.
18. Formulation of alternatives is essential as a retention strategy.
19. Evaluation and comparison of the alternatives helps consumer decision taking.
20. Markets like civilizations grow, mature, decline and sometimes fall.
21. Some players are too big to fail.
22. Some players become too big and become dinosaurs. Bigger organizations tend to be mammoth, complex, and are prone to bureaucracy and grow impersonal. They may be inert.
23. Consumers think markets in terms of products and services earning power and future cash flows.
24. B2B is important in buying. Markets of today exact the emergence of large organizations, which have economies of scale.
25. Do something different: can we offer a lower priced product; or can we give the customer

more benefits? Customers like more for less; we cannot be more or less organizations.

26. Small could be beautiful but not necessarily bountiful. Customers are aware that economies of scale are advantageous to them. Customers form cartels as much as the providers of goods and services do. Power play becomes crucial.
27. The percentage of market that you command is crucial for your decisions.
28. A challenge to your competitor must be credible.
29. If you are large enough you could fend off competition. If your competitor is as big as you then possible he would 'hit and run' in a contestable market.
30. In transient periods, organizations have to destroy ideas, practices and rewrite organizational structures to meet the challenge of the new customer.
31. Today's organizations are arrays of partners. Garner forces or form a grand coalition to do a well-knit, integrated marketing.
32. There is a need to collectively learn and to collectively unlearn tactics.

33. Old management practices are no longer so valid; there may have to be an abandoning of the narrower practices.
34. An organization must gain knowledge of the drivers of change: these driving forces draw in new profit and sculpt long-term buyer behavior.
35. Being on a 'learning curve' is significant to success. A marketer can afford to be indifferent only if one is a monopoly seller. In real world, such monopsony does not exist. Even Microsoft has to recognize that it is not the monarch of all that it surveys.
36. Today's markets in most products and services are moving to a demand and supply inspired near perfect markets. The best example is the foreign exchange market
37. Organizations need to have an agenda for the future. Organizational reflexes matter: tactics make a difference; the intensity of competition trend will push prices downwards.
38. Competitors may strategically cut prices to retain market shares. In a market of few sellers, it is natural that when one cuts, the

other has to follow suit. That leaves the consumer at an advantage.

39. Price hara-kiri (self-destruction) will ultimately result in serious damage to at least a few sellers and to all sellers to some extent.

40. In a buyer's market, where the consumer has seized the initiative, prices will fall. Middle rungs will go; the membrane between the wholesaler and the retailer will thin.

41. In a market of falling prices, who makes the most in the least time is the one that proves the tactical effectiveness of managers.

42. Critical positioning is important. Positioning is about occupying a place in the mind of the selected consumer or group of consumers.

43. The organization is to be perceived by the customer as having positioned through the vision of its top management, the excellence its staff and the standards of efficiency it sets for itself.

44. If you are perceived as immune to change, then your organization is branded static.

45. Competition is real time.

46. Competitors might be too powerful. The weak lament. The wise are not disturbed. Only the serene can stay.
47. Competitors might malign products indirectly. This is painful to receive; do not respond in kind.
48. You need to lift your morale high in the face of aggressive competition. You need to be determined. Warriors do not flee the battlefield—they fight.
49. Never underestimate your opponents; rather treat them respectfully.
50. Do not grieve over a lost customer. Remember this is the battlefield of competition. Loss of business is common here.
51. You should not allow any attachment to a state of inactivity even if you have performed well to achieve the budgeted targets.
52. You should not rest on your oars; there might be a tide on its wavy way. If one rests in the battlefield, then the competitor might render the opponent as incompetent to fight.
53. Every action has an equal and vehement reaction. The competitor will match your

move. If you cut prices, he will follow. If you raise, he may not follow.
54. Every object continues in a state of inertia until one applies force on it. One has to gently pressurize the non-customer into action in a tactical move to wean him away from his present organization.
55. Triggers are important. Somebody has to awaken the spirit in the customer. Trigger the customer with great service. The marketer needs to be on a high himself and keep the customer in state of euphoria.
56. Pyramid deals are the ideal strategy in competition. Neither the Egyptians nor the Romans did all in a day. Build your profits over time.
57. In and out trading is better than a long wait for "great kill".
58. The wild cats wait long observing the herd of its prey; they kill the weakest. That is the practitioner's market. They position themselves and observe before they leap for the kill. Positioning is thus important and is vital in tactics.

59. Pygmalion Effect[1] is important in competition. Believe that you are powerful enough to negate competition and you will.
60. Belief systems need to be supported by perseverance.
61. Do not fall in love with your strategy or your tactics. There could be some serious flaws there. Your competitor is eternally sharpening his skills. You have to review at periodical frequency depending on the intensity of the conflict.
62. The productive worker is growing older in old economies.
63. New economies have large populations.
64. Population is demand. Market sizes are important.
65. In the buyer driven market of today, wages and costs must remain competitive. If costs are not pushed down, there will have to be

---

[1] *"... the difference between a lady and a flower girl is not how she behaves, but how she's treated. I shall always be a flower girl to Professor Higgins, because he always treats me as a flower girl, and always will; but I know I can be a lady to you, because you always treat me as a lady, and always will".* (George Bernard Shaw)

a migration of organizations to lowly priced centres.

66. Outsourcing affects markets.
67. Sustaining competitive advantage is a grim task.
68. In days of recession, protectionism of nationalistic corporate is attempted by Governments.
69. Corporate mergers help meet market challenges. Size matters today for both organizations and trade blocs.
70. Mergers and strategic alliances augment market size but may increase risk appetites. Mere mergers of systems may only sweep inefficiencies to the carpet.
71. The market can be buoyed by sentiment or consumer confidence.
72. Government spending decisions have trendiest impacting even in a privatized world.
73. Any flow of funds into the system is a welcome sign for the market as it enhances purchasing power. Markets thrive on people's ability to spend and their willingness to spend.

74. An overhang of liquidity may actually push down purchasing power.
75. Clients abhor inflation.
76. Markets function within constraint systems. You have to deliver within the given framework; not by attempting to remove the constraints.
77. Vested interest groups remain a major barrier to reform in any market. In free economies, such groups could be the mega corporations. In smaller economies, it could be the existence of big corporate families. These interests attempt to smother competition.
78. You cannot wish vested interests away. You have to work within the limits set by the system, as it exists.
79. Bureaucracy hurts economics: lack of accountability and transparency affect the overall growth pattern. This is a given quantum. Cribbing about it will not solve it. You have to work with them as you cannot destroy them but they can destroy you.
80. Culture may constrain or accelerate growth. Either way, it influences. Good strategists

recognize this, not ignore it. Different groups approach purchases differently.

81. A feeling of superiority in you at any point of time during an interaction is arrogance. Ethnocentrism in marketing is abominable.

82. Sometimes organizational systems, of which you are a part, may be under 'convoy' carrying along the weakest link.

83. The system might discourage an open debate and allow special interests to block needed changes. A marketer is a leader: a leader does not shy away from problems but is a leader as he solves them.

84. Change management is a good strategy, however as a practitioner, you recognize that change may not be immediate. Dramatic re-engineering may be difficult in organizations unless there is great will power; what oft occurs is incremental change. Strategy works best on recognition of reality.

85. The lifetime employment system does not exist any more except in feeble organizations. So tactics are needed to keep your profit targets on.

86. 'In the long run', as Keynes said, 'we are all dead'. So the strategy has to base itself on the bunch of tactics that organizations have. Many short-term equilibrium points make a long-term equilibrium. Short-term tactics may fall into a pattern of a long-term delivery strategy.
87. Corporate governance based on market principles requires according the customer the status of a stakeholder. Stakeholder analysis is crucial in strategy.
88. One has to discern the various types of purchasers: some are active buyers, some early birds, some followers, some mere bystanders waiting, watching what really happens, some are senior policy makers: a whole host of people that really have a say in your marketing effort. You have to balance.
89. You could misread your opponent.
90. There are asymmetries among firms.
91. There could be reaction lags; or detection lags.
92. Factors affecting markets would be bulk orders; hidden or incomplete information; volatility of demand conditions.

93. You could lead on quality or on service or on cost.
94. You could be a product specialist.
95. You could have a single niche or a multiple niche or a mass market strategy.
96. Every product and market pass through the stages of take off, growth, maturity and decline.
97. Presume that Product life cycle is short.

Book of Trends

1. Build your brand. Communicate your brand.
2. Brand renders you premium. Suit the brand to the trend.
3. Trend changes are consequential to today's 'globalized village' concept:
4. Identify broad trends and assess their impact on consumer think: recession, weaker Europe, the rise of Asia, the price of oil, trade blocs like the European Union, the North American Free Trade Association, the Association of South East Asian Nations etc.
5. The quantum leap of education;
6. The inevitability of information technology;
7. De-ruralization and urbanization;
8. De localization and enhanced indidualization;
9. The gradual retreat of the baby-boomer segment;

10. The rise of the consumption hungry middle classes particularly in Asia and the newly transient Europe;
11. A politically insecure society (where 'fear creates its own ghosts which are more fearsome than fear itself')
12. A receding industrial economy;
13. The emergence of the tertiary sector with the dominance of services;
14. Industrial powers of yester year in Europe and Americas under threat of losing economic power;
15. The rise of population mammoth economies like China and India on the economic horizon;
16. The money powered few countries;
17. Uncertainties of an aging society where medicine perpetuates the customer;
18. Contrasting trends in birthrate;
19. An environment-friendly society;
20. Significant influence of religion on market thinking;
21. Technology gap narrowing down between you and the competitor.
22. Digitalization;

23. Miniaturization;
24. In a growing market, competitor may not mind your enhanced growth as he also receives a share of the cake.
25. In a mature market, the market share tends to be stagnant.
26. 'Just in time' is the philosophy for supply management.

Book VII

Finer Points for Competition and the Marketer

1. Dress to kill. Package well—pack to attract.
2. Differentiate. Make it difficult to imbibe. Switching costs may not hold back a customer if value is greater.
3. Afford some risks. Be prudent in selecting risks.
4. Assess your market share in relative terms—to your competitor. The larger the share, the stronger you are.
5. Your product is not immortal. Sell it fast.
6. Every product on your shelf or in your show room or in your warehouse has a four stage life cycle: there is an introductory phase; then it grows; it peaks to mature and then declines. Try to keep it going.
7. Keep your brand identity.
8. Interact sincerely and continuously.

9. Engage your customer so that he recalls you at every need.
10. Personalize your customer. Own him.
11. Lead your customer.
12. Welcome him to your fold. Strategize to keep him with simple words of tactical gratitude. Emails cost near nothings.
13. Cajole your customer to share information about himself; persuade him to buy; encourage him to give you a greater share of his wallet.
14. Organize your system around your customer.
15. Push out your product
16. Pull in your customer.
17. Substitutes await round the corner.
18. Buyers are willing to experiment. Involve them.
19. In evolving strategy and in solutions, simple steps are the easiest to handle and retain clients.
20. Have a good well integrated system to know your customer.

21. Define every problem, every goal, and every issue painstakingly together with the customer.
22. Meet with your colleagues in strategy formulation, as the task is too big to be done single handedly.
23. You believe sometimes that you have ready-made mix of answer. Do not assume things away.
24. Do not fall in love with your inventory. Hoarding is unprofessional. Remember your task is to sell them earliest; beautiful stocks do not enhance your showroom.
25. Do not generalize. Do not focus too narrowly either.
26. Be realistic and pragmatic in all your assessment. All good managers are practical people.
27. Be always inspired by all around and inspire all around.
28. Customers like high—impact blitz campaigns, which are harmless but enticing. Customers see visual media more than read the print media today.

29. The image campaign of your organization needs radical changes. Customers enjoy ad seizures. Media plans need to eschew the traditional route.
30. Brand competition is followed intensely. People like promotional aggression, which does not affect them. Some customers may even like it a bit weird.
31. Building or simulating a futuristic scenario is important.
32. Visibility is important to attract the customer. You might take hits on prices just to stay visible. Visibility increases chances of relationship.
33. If your organization retains, on average, 90% of existing customers in any given year, remember that these clients together with the minority of defectors from your competitor will bestow you a significant percent of your profits in the future.
34. Distribution outlets are thinning out with rapid technological advancement. Bricks no longer make a branch.
35. The net is here to revolutionize. It still, however, remains that a larger network of

showrooms or branches brings in economies as much as customer reassurance. It heightens visibility and after sales' service capabilities.

36. Companies and institutions, which are successful today, are those in the throes of change. You need to be highly motivated and trained to bring about change.

37. The market is the driver; most organizations are only travellers; very few can alter the direction or the pace. Even supra-national organizations like the International Monetary Fund or the World Bank find that changing the course of events is difficult in the immediate near period.

38. Innovations in product-offers have shrunk the world; Darwinian competition has given rise to the emergence of new products.

39. Maintaining competitiveness means that organizations keep running. You have to keep running to keep walking.

40. Consumers become more exacting in modern scenario and organizations have to be more than just responsive. You have to be proactive to manage customer business.

41. There is a paradoxical fear in the minds of most marketing personnel that market shares may dry up. As societies become more progressive, customer loyalty may decline.
42. Several of today's customers are silent; they may observe and pick up new products but may not be quite expressive in the traditional sense of their needs. The future is thus going to be different; customer preferences may not be very predictable. Today's technological and entrepreneurial urges must ensure that commercial applications are packaged customer friendly.
43. Businesses are intensely aware of this. The new customers will usually, be more educated and aware than the older segment; the degree of satiation for them will have to be of a higher order. The degree of impatience with the current customer will be more. The level of assertion will also be more.
44. In any circumstances, you are not to be seen leading the customer. Your role is to act as a facilitator.
45. Think ahead of the customer and create new products and services for the; then you are

not leading the customer to it but following his desires.

46. The successful companies are those that pleasantly surprise the customer with the new product or service.
47. Competition leads to a higher productivity curve. Respond to competition with an awareness-building programme that tells employees of probable problems.
48. Rework your strategies Rework your thoughts. Rework your employees to higher performance levels. Only the best hold out in history. The rest are unsung.
49. Create a deep sense of productive urgency.
50. Unleash competitive vitality in you. If you are unenthused or unconvinced, you cannot enthuse or convince the client.

Book VIII

Buyer Psychology

'The desire to be admired is very powerful'
Bertrand Russell

1. Customer behavior is an ever—dynamic process. It may appear to be erratic at times.
2. Customers react to a plethora of choices, which are available.
3. Some customers are more cautious in decision taking. Some purchasers are more circumspect, they appear to be doubting toms.
4. There are times when customers take quite measured steps. These are times when they tend to be more motivated by the ensuing purchase: they are more involved. They are measured except when they buy items where they are not quite involved. Giving them time to arrive at a choice is essential.

5. Customers shift products and occasionally even buying behaviour as they respond to marketing initiatives.
6. Customers search. Alternatives flow to them from all around.
7. A decision is a judgment for the customer. It is a choice between alternatives. The customer doubts the decision: it is at best a choice that oscillates between absolutely appropriate to more appropriate to inappropriate to a mis-judgement. The consumer may be unsure.
8. The consumer is influenced by cultural, social, psychological and personal factors.
9. Consumer is influenced by family.
10. Buyers are influenced by technical aspects and technicians.
11. Customers huddle and herd together in formations of affinity, aspiration or in dis-associative lots.
12. Customers may exhibit lack of belongingness in their approach. All flux in a consumer's mind arises from his anticipation and consequential uncertainty.

13. The mind, the intellect and the ego of the customer are all horses at great swift strides. The marketer may either add to the confusion or clarify; his role is to clarify.
14. The client observes, thinks, elicits opinion, obtains facts, mentally develops solution scenarios, screens the given set of options, sets controls and then accepts what he considers to be the best judgment in given circumstances. The consumer is always thus a learner.
15. Experience emphatically conditions a consumer. Consumers always like to know, sometimes they think that they know, and occasionally act at various points of time
16. Consumers grade attachment or risk or both to assess the need of their involvement in the purchase decision.
17. Once the purchase is made, the consumer sometimes hears sounds contrary to their beliefs, attitudes or values. Post purchase, client's anxiety levels do rise. The more expensive the purchase, the more the discomforting sounds reach them. The marketer has to reinvigorate the customer

and renew faith in the deal; reassurance is then essential for the client. The marketer has a role to play here: that of a leadership character role. As Jan Carlson said, the task of a leader is to eloquently set forth values and to create a system in which people can be productive. There is need for reinforcement of the faith system in the customer.

18. 'Support your customer and he becomes supportive of you'. When the marketer gives away to his customer, he is not destroying he is not even preserving but he is creating something new.

19. The marketer needs to exalt his customer; he needs to elevate him to a higher plateau by genuine effort. The customer shall and should stay at a platonic higher level. He passes the message of goodwill references around.

20. Customer has a natural tendency to be loyal. There should be no reason given to him to be disloyal. Your bestowal of attention must be such that you afford him no opportunity even for a momentary fling.

21. Customers might get a seizure to switch or flee. It could arise out of boredom or the excitement of trying something new. Give no opportunity for a switch over. Offer him new products to keep him hooked onto you.
22. Some customers spend to overcome stress. Customers feel melancholic occasionally. Be aware of mood swings.
23. Customers feel powerless at abject negativism strewn around when we criticize our competitors. Rather than criticism, a buyer prefers stimulus from your stories and your actions. Consumers prefer straightforward deals.
24. Being in touch post purchase keeps him happy. The customer's near and dear ones might abet post purchase anxiety: mitigate his anxiety through reassurance.
25. Customers, being intensely human, value their egos and time. Organizations have to condition the product deliverer to this psychology. The employee has to be aware that the past is sometimes an indicator of the future.

26. Customers prefer to be orderly. They often think that periodic rearranging items on shelves in a departmental store are a time-waster; they would rather prefer arrangements to be like a library where books are available according to the index.
27. When the jobless rate is high, the citizen is overtaken by unemployment anxiety. Recession numbs the customer. Fear of job loss tends to adversely affect the savings-spending-investment cycle. The private individual may keep all his savings in liquid form, even given the fact that interest rates are at low levels. There is a retraction from spending much ahead of any actual reduction in the disposable incomes. The demand for goods and services then declines affecting real income levels: the market has goods that do not sell. Pessimism is infectious.
28. The demographic structure of population affects. Young people borrow to buy. As they move towards middle ages, they pay back the loans and buy more classy items. As they move up the social ladder over a time frame, buying pattern undergoes change.

29. 'Keeping up with the Joneses' matter. There is conspicuous consumption, and consumers are affected by demonstration effect. Some traders take advantage of the human flaw of vanity and sell products that are beyond the financial capacity of the consumer. This is amoral perhaps: making money at cost of the ignorant is not worth pursuing a career on.
30. As they grow into mature, senior citizens, the purchase decisions may seem ideal but apprehension of future spending streams sets in. Reassurance again is the key.
31. Consumers like to stick together; they are birds together flying away from the winter of life. They are like elephants where the only the rogue elephant breaks ranks. The rest conform.

Book IX

On the Marketer-Psyche: Of Hope and Fear

'It takes humility to seek feedback'
—Stephen Covey

1. Marketing is among the most specialized of functions. The marketer represents a band of business-spinning professionals who constitute the core of 'profit-related activity' in any organization.
2. A good marketer while being an extrovert works away from the gaze of the public, a recluse deep in knowledge. His active shoulder is on a continual update mode: his objective: to make most while the trend moves in his direction.
3. A marketer is an ebullient, enthusiastic and a daring knight: the organization has reposed a lot of confidence in the abilities to charge forward. It has perhaps vested financial

muscle under the delegation of powers. The Marketer is enabled, energized and empowered to trade in the market. All this the organization has done, in anticipation that all the Marketer's skills will be turned to a competitive advantage for the organization.

4. Organizations are profit bodies, not charity joints. They expect the Marketer to add to their bottom lines. There is thus quite a bit of pressure on the Marketer to perform.

5. The rapidity of the Marketer's reflexes and the business acumen are exploited by the organization to its advantage. Thus organizations and the marketer have an exchange relationship.

6. The Marketer receives information through men and machines and inputs the information as throughput in his systems, which assist the Marketer, generate output to a purpose. Customer Information File, Management Information System, Executive Information Systems all are updated on a continuum.

7. The Marketer is aware that the manner of handling the internal and internal external transactions can influence substantially the

organizational business, customer relations and the annual profit figures.
8. That is the hope. But boundaries are drawn by the organization: there are limits to his market dealings.
9. The market views any transgression with dis-favour; organizations also do not view with favour any trended losses. That is the fear too.
10. So the Marketer has to work out a neat balancing act between hope for the best and fear for the worst.
11. Self-indoctrination is vital for survival. Culling out information from among the several commentaries on the markets is crucial. Trend movements and competitor movements are both crucial.
12. Loss is an enemy the Marketer will retreat from; there is need to cut-loss.
13. Group dynamics is important in marketing. In a marketing team there is a fellow feeling and commonality of interests that binds together amidst the heat of intense competition. Your enemy's enemy is your friend. The Marketer's colleagues are the competitor's enemy.

14. Market is sometimes a zero-sum game: someone has to lose for someone to gain.
15. Alertness has to be supplemented with tracking down of all the key fundamental or economic factors. Speeches and views of economists, key Government personnel; market commentaries all matter of significance.
16. The periodic release of a plethora of data; the political occurrences in the key areas of the world; trend patterns made out on the basis of innumerable observations made in the historical past and attempts to predict what are the probable future movements are all keys to success.
17. Seasonality is an attribute of marketing.
18. Information is indeed power but it is the Marketer's ability to interpret information that is more crucial. On the basis of the information that marketers obtain, they form viewpoints.
19. Mere information is not power, because technological sophistication ensures that all in the market and your competitors, receive the same information at the same time. The

knowledge basis you have always puts you at an advantage or otherwise.
20. Bigger players in the market have a lot more resources. Size matters.
21. Client Sentiments matter. In an uncertain world, clan feelings run strong: customers buy or bunk a model together.
22. The market is too big a place for anyone to individually influence. You are to follow trends on the premise that the majority thinks alike. So if one sells, others sell too. The herd instinct in people is strong. Few would fall out of line. The fear of losing in stepping out of the Group line is gripping.
23. The trend formed is to be followed. Contrarian trends are not always successful.
24. The marketer cannot hope to end up with a success ratio of 100 percent of all the deals he or she undertakes. Seasoned veterans may agree that a fairer estimate may be that a good marketer makes his good profits in most times but there are lean times too! The profits that he makes in the deals that are profitable must be of such volumes as to cover up for the losses of those few that he lost out on.

25. The marketer's internal tension levels tend to be quite high in a deal and the customer's even more so.
26. The volatility of the market is an exciting opportunity but nothing is worth busting management and prudential norms. Not even fat bonuses give one a right to so do. Values and ethics are core points on which a marketer's inner strengths lie.
27. The essentials of the build up in this psyche are thus: be watchful in parts, be daring in greater measure and oscillate between hope and fear—hope for the best possible rate and fear for the worst possible commotion in the marketplace. Internal controls and external checks should keep occasional over-ambition and greed at bay.

Book X

The Learning Marketer

'You shall listen to all sides and filter them from yourself'.

Walt Whitman

1. The donor cannot give the recipient more than he has, so if you are not knowledgeable then you cannot part with information.
2. This is the era of 'a *knowledge worker*' as Peter Drucker pointed out.
3. If you are true, then you ought to present yourself as proficient and professional.
4. All professionalism comes from a continuum of learning.
5. Learning is experience. Experience is learning.
6. In customer dealings be self-controlled rather than sense controlled. Do not retaliate even when provoked.

7. The ideal marketer is the objective marketer; he is objective unduly to his deal or the person behind the deal. He who is objective to a transaction yet involved in it has set himself on the established path to wisdom.
8. Core competence in marketing is the collective marketing wisdom of your organization.
9. Ask yourself if your organization has core competence to support your delivery. You are only a competence carrier.
10. Rely on strong points of the organization but do not overlook the weak. Integrity is the hallmark of a good marketer.
11. It is unethical to take undue advantage of the client. Conscientious performance relaxes the mind and the soul.
12. Give yourself a tool to compete: it could be personal mastery, personality, or your warmth. There must be something in you, which you can capitalize on.
13. Guard with utmost confidentiality what is inscribed in the customer information file.
14. Know that truth prevails. Absolute truth prevails absolutely.

15. Encourage austerity in your customer. His savings today are added spending for you tomorrow.
16. Have faith in your internal customer and in your product.
17. Concentrate on the person and the transaction in equal measure.
18. Understanding might mean sacrifice-of your time, of your convenience. Sacrifice is bliss in relationship.
19. For a client, you symbolize all essential characteristics: perception, understanding, knowledge, wisdom, inspiration, thinking resolution and sacrifice. Your customer does not expect you to have feet of clay. People who lack confidence cannot convince others. Clients do not stick to losers.
20. The client follows memory. Learning on firsthand experience lays the foundation of a relationship.
21. Do not carry yourself as a non-performer.
22. Have possible multi-channel communication conduits to your customer.
23. Recognize dissatisfaction decibels. Hear the whisper. Hear that which is inaudible.

24. Be receptive in action. Listening means nothing to the customer if not translated to service.
25. Respect the power of findings of research. Look at these findings in depth: you may be able to see what the others could not.
26. You would accept that internal customers are as much stakeholders as the shareholders in the success of the organization.
27. Customers want to improve their own quality: assisting them in this task is your task.
28. Knit an integrated framework to sustain yourself and your customer.
29. Get honest information about customer problems. Do not go by third party views unless they are so dependable. Good managers verify what they hear.
30. Free yourself from the attachment to results. Attachment causes tension.
31. The beginning is: KYC: know your customer well.
32. Communication cements knowing.
33. Thought is essential in communication.

34. Communication establishes relationship.
35. Awareness ignites communication and deep reflection.
36. Understanding is consequential to reflection and all action emanates from such understanding.
37. Action alone satisfies the customer in the long run.
38. Markets are exciting places to work in.
39. Ignorance is sin in marketing.
40. Be calm and detached in dedication to the customer.
41. The marketer must perform his duties faithfully and a sense of devotion.
42. There is no one approach to a customer; there is no uniform approach in marketing. The market is multi-dimensional. Success is in knitting the various threads together.
43. Success is a one point Manifesto: Meet and satiate client needs to his delight. The rest follows.
44. The marketer must attempt to be genuine and authentic; to have Character; Vision; Will; and Wisdom.

45. All efforts should be to meet virtuous standards. All good marketers have a deep sense of yearning for knowledge.
46. The marketer is nowhere without training and education.
47. One must recognize that confidence[2] is essential.
48. They paint best who are deeply sensitive. They paint best who are outside the given canvas.
49. They are best who are catalysts to the growth of the customer.
50. Successful people evolve transparent systems so that there is a discernible feel of fair play.
51. Money matters but not so much as priceless service.
52. The client, in his perception, does he perceive you as a friend? Does he use adjectives such as dependable; reliable; predictable; consistent; caring; empathetic; duty bound; sincere; strong character; value driven; integrity biased; loyalty inducing? (for you).

---

[2] 'Winners', as Khera said, 'don't do different things, they do things differently'.

Are these descriptions of yours? Earn them through your deeds.

53. The market is moving: moving towards controlled deregulation and may over a period move towards de-supervision. That thrusts the onus of responsibility more on the marketer than ever before. The more autonomous he is the more responsible he has to be.

54. Empowerment is crucial in today's scenario. Empowerment of the internal customer (the employee) means help him being proactive; keeping the purpose of the relationship in mind; setting out things in the right priority; seeking to think Win-Win; seeking first to understand; then to be understood; emphasizing on synergies being derived out of the communion between the organization and the customer; sharpening mental, spiritual, physical and social areas; emotionally reassuring the customer.

55. Bargaining power is a decisive factor in transactions. Ruthless power games mean temporary success.

56. The customer is not to be overawed but impressed gently.
57. Do not rejoice that your competitor did not meet his targets. It perhaps is an early warning signal: it indicates a stalling market.
58. Work is Commitment. Every experience for a marketer is a humbling, learning event. The subtle essence of the existence of an organization is the customer. One who knows this is endowed with the golden light. This is the truth. This is what is real.
59. The customer must see you, think you, comprehend you and trust you.

www.ingramcontent.com/pod-product-compliance
Lightning Source LLC
Chambersburg PA
CBHW022122170526
45157CB00004B/1717